T_____

Fr___ackie
       &
    Taryn !! :)

Other giftbooks by Helen Exley:
If it's cute and crazy it must be MY CAT!
Glorious Cats   Cat Quotations

To my wonderful assistant Amelia – a.k.a. Mamma, from Maria

Published simultaneously in 1997 by Exley Publications in Great Britain, and Exley
Giftbooks in the USA.
Copyright © Helen Exley 1997
Illustrations © Maria Teresa Meloni 1977
Edited by Helen Exley

12 11 10 9 8 7 6 5 4 3 2 1

Illustrations by Maria Teresa Meloni
Written by Pam Brown

ISBN 1-85015-851-7

Designed by Pinpoint Design.
Typeset by Delta, Watford.
Printed in China.

Acknowledgements: Alessandro Dianda, Cat Breeder, Viareggio, Italy – for supply of the
"models"; Renzo de Benedetti (il Signor Palombaro); Renata Vitelli; La Cuccia, Cat
Shelter, Viareggio, Italy.

Exley Publications Ltd, 16 Chalk Hill, Watford, Herts WD1 4BN, UK.
Exley Giftbooks, 232 Madison Avenue, Suite 1206, NY 10016, USA.

Kittens!

EXLEY

NEW YORK • WATFORD, UK

LOVE ME, PLEASE

Round, misty-blue eyes
stare desperately
from the wicker basket.
Love me, they say, feed me, warm me,
care for me, let me into your life –
so that I can begin to take over
your entire existence.

PLAYTIME

For a kitten

the world

is an enchantment.

A challenge.

The best thing that God

ever did for kittens was to

invent string.

PERFECTION

There is no yawn
as pink and clean
and set with pin sharp teeth
as that of a kitten.

Even Fabergé
could never
have fashioned something
as exquisite
in its detail
as a tiny kitten.

The hands of a human baby fascinate – but a
kitten's paws seem scarcely possible.
So small, so delicate, so beautifully made.
Fur neat and nice.
Claws needle sharp.
Pads pristine and pink as roses.
Touching, discouraging, manipulating.
Scampering and pattering.
Swinging and clinging,
climbing and scrabbling.
Folding softly over little faces
lost in sleep.

A SHIVERING SCRAP edges from the cat basket, and vanishes behind the sofa. "Poor little soul," they say.
"Perhaps a little plaice. A little milk."
"Don't startle her."
By morning she has scattered food across the kitchen. Established a bed in the linen basket. Removed the vegetables from the rack. Shredded a roll of toilet paper. Climbed the lace curtains – to their detriment. Walked milk into the passage.
Used her box – with a vigorous displacement of the litter.
And fallen asleep on the stove.
She wakes and beams at the first man down.
"I like it here," she signals.
"How about a game of string?"

WHERE'S THE KITTEN?

All over the world a game is being
played – Where's the Kitten?
Chinese, Japanese, Norwegians, Swiss,
Italians, Arabs, British and Americans
– all on their knees, peering under
furniture.
Kitty! Kitty! Kitty! in a hundred
tongues – and a universal sigh of relief
when the little cat emerges – from the
one place it could not possibly be.

Kitten owners learn never to discount
the impossible.
They look under the car before
starting the engine.
Shut no drawers or doors without a
double check
(and this includes ovens and washing
machines).
Never nail down a floorboard or close
an attic without the kitten in full view.

There is no such thing as an
ordinary kitten.

Who will this little kitten be?
A tough old Tomcat with a heart
of gold; an opportunist thief;
a sprawler in the sun; an acrobat;
a sentimental smuggler; a wise
philosopher; a charming half-wit;
a devisor of games;
an untangler of puzzles?
Who knows? Perhaps
a combination of them all.
But always special.
Always a marvel.

WHO'S THE BOSS?

A kitten has a minuscule paw.
Yet within two weeks he has the entire
household firmly under it.

A cat allows you to sleep on the bed.
On the edge.

Kittens take us in hand
very soon in their lives.
They tug us down to a height where
they can spring up to our shoulders.
They tell us how to unlock kitchen
doors. They summon us to play.
They sulk if put down from our knees.
They hog the bed.

A KITTEN IS A PROMISE

*A kitten is like a baby. It gives no hint
of what's to come....
A blink of the eye and this tiny,
staggering creature, falling from chairs
and getting tied up in the Newton
Cradle, is elegance itself, leaping
nonchalantly from roof to roof,*

swaying on the oak tree's topmost
bough, a hunter, a dancer in the wind.
Kittens and babies are an amazement
and delight.
But the best lies hidden in the future.

A kitten is only a beginning.
A funny, ingenious, lovable beginning –
but only a promise of the cat to come.

THERE IS NOTHING SO BOLD and venturesome
as a climbing kitten.
There is nothing so pitiful as one who is stuck.

KITTENS TAKE infinite pleasure in climbing to the
very top of the trees and teetering there, their little
pink mouths wide with panic, their pitiful cries
bringing out the people along the street. In a
scrabble of leaves and twigs they cling and sway –
while someone fetches the ladder from the shed
and lugs it to the spot. At which point the kitten
leaps down and races off – climbs to an even
higher vantage point and starts the game again.

LOVELY LITTLE DESTRUCTION MACHINES!

Kittens and curtains.
One must choose which one loves
the most.

No burr can cling as fast as a kitten to
an exceedingly expensive sweater.

Kittens are made wide-eyed, fluffy,
pink-mouthed, winsome.
These attributes are what lie
between them and extinction when
they have ripped the new lace curtains
into shreds.

There are quiet, shy, gentle kittens,
worried, nervous kittens,
comic kittens,
bold as brass, take-on-the-world kittens,
gormless, muddle-headed kittens,
clever kittens.
Kittens with a chip on their shoulder
and a tendency to sulk.
And all beautiful.
And all needing a human being
who will think them the very best
kitten in the universe.

PRIDE

A cross kitten is a sight to see. He comes across the room sideways, on tiptoe, burning with rage – his fur on end, his tail a bottle brush, whiskers bristling, mouth wide, huffing with rage.

At all costs do not laugh at him.

A kitten has his pride.

The lesson a kitten learns early

in its life is:

When you fall off, over, through

or out of anything,

look as though it was intentional.

A pup likes to be laughed at.

The smallest kitten is mortally offended.

CHAOS!   BEDLAM!
PANDEMONIUM!

To a grown cat, water is for drinking,
pellets are for eating.
To a kitten water and pellets are for
flicking, splashing,
dabbling and rummaging.
Leaving the kitchen resembling a
public beach at low tide.

One day the kittens are in the box with their mama, blind and helpless, available for inspection and the admiration of everyone. The next thing they are off adventuring – swinging from the curtains, ascending the Eiger of the bookcase, rummaging in the clothes basket, eating the potted plants, dancing on the piano, skidding across the polished table, digging in the window-box.

Three kittens transmagnified to thirty.

IN NEED OF PITY

A wet kitten is one of the most pitiful
sights on earth.

It's a hard heart a kitten cannot melt.

*It doesn't matter if you are six feet
four and broad of shoulder, if a kitten
is looking for a mother figure —
you're it.*

CATS RULE THE WORLD

A kitten learns from its mother
the Great Secret.
That cats rule the world.

You may out-think your kitten
once or twice –
but he learns, my friend, he learns.

A very small kitten wanting possession
of a very large chair – gets it.

Those couples who acquire a kitten
for the first time,
go to a lot of trouble
to make it a cosy bed
in the kitchen.
Only to wake up to find it sleeping
peacefully between them.

The smallest kitten
only needs a week
to be in full possession
of a house and its owners.

*There is only one way
to survive a kitten.
Learn to speak Cat.
Fast.*

*There is nothing so down-putting as
an exasperated kitten who has failed to
explain something to you, despite
putting it in words of one syllable.*

HUMANS ARE IDIOTS!

A KITTEN WILL imagine a piece of paper on a string to be a mouse, until you enter into the spirit of the game. It will then regard you as a lunatic, and take to washing its paws.

❧

A kitten is often exasperated by the half-wittedness of humans, but lives in hope that with time, patience and affection, it will be able to instill a little sense into them.

A puppy loves to learn, to please,
to be rewarded.
"Come," we say, "Sit. Beg. Heel. Play dead."
And they are overcome by our
congratulations.
A kitten listens. Smiles.
Says "Come. Sit. Fetch. Keep still."
And we obey.

🐾

All kittens, from the very first, set out to
teach their humans to adapt to the needs of a
cat. As a reward, they grant them the
position of honorary cat.

A cat so small
he sits secure upon your hand,
his paws white daisies,
his eyes still misted
with the blue
of babyhood.
And yet – he curls
his skimpy tail about him,
regal as any ancient Beast,
lifts his head,
surveys his universe.
For he is totally aware
that he is Cat.

H O U D I N I ?

The kitten's lost. Panic through the household. Open every door. Open every drawer. Search under, over and behind. No sign. No sound. And then – suddenly – he's there. Watching you all with puzzled interest.

Kittens fit in nicely where reason declares no kitten could fit.

Life is never
dull if you are fortunate enough
to acquire an imaginative kitten.
Every light pull, latch and paper bag
becomes transformed
into a source of new invention.
Every pot, pan, row of books and laundry
basket is a hiding place.
Every shut drawer, door and box has
a secret entrance.
Houdini? Pouff!

A very small kitten in a vet's waiting room
attracts all eyes – the owners of Afghans, bull
terriers, chinchillas, guinea pigs and rats all
turn to focus on the scrap of fur.
"Aah," they say, "The little dear."
At which the kitten, spotting the largest of
the dogs, raises itself on tiptoe, fluffs out its
fur, lays back its ears and hisses, revealing
two rows of tiny teeth. The largest dog is
utterly amazed. And with a show of
nonchalance, looks the other way.
The very small kitten subsides, relaxes.
Having settled the question of authority.

IT'S ALL A MATTER OF TACTICS...

A kitten learns early these lessons
instilled in it by its mama.
Never make messes indoors, other
than in one's cat box.
Be sick, however, absolutely anywhere.
Nowhere is off limits.
Never sleep in a cat bed
if you can find a lap.

The food you adored last week
is not necessarily the food
you will even sniff at this week.
Refuse it totally.
If necessary, go through
the ritual of covering it up
with imaginary earth.
Never spend the night
in the kitchen
if you can get the bedroom
door open.
When in trouble, resort to
The Silent Meow.

AN INNOCENT KITTEN?

Kittens learn early
to listen intently
when someone calls them –
and do absolutely
nothing.

How innocent a kitten's eyes.
How devious its soul!

THE KITTENS ARE BORN

Kittens come gift-wrapped,
neat packages of life.
Most delicately mama removes the tissue –
and reveals a blind and stump-eared
mewling and tousled promise of perfection,
paws small as daisies, stripes
fine as pencil strokes.
She is astonished –
but accepts this extraordinary change,
licks them into order,

tidies her nest and, still bemused,

settles to feed them.

"Look what I've done,"

her great eyes say.

"What an astonishment." And turns to wash

the nearest butting head.

*T*here's a look on a mother cat's face

that any new human mother

will recognize...

exasperated bewilderment

combined with loving pride.

A LIFETIME BOND

The small, sad kitten
that needed to be buttoned
into one's cardigan and carried,
papoose-fashion, about the house,
is the kitten that,
a week later,
is rampaging joyfully
from room to room.
But the bond is made —
and will last a lifetime.

A pup is taught that its duty
in life is to find a human
being to serve and to love.
A kitten is taught to find an
adaptable and affectionate
slave who will respond
to kindness.

A very large man.
A man of muscle,
of power, of energy.
Sitting very, very still.
Breathing very, very quietly.
A kitten the size of a teacup
is sleeping in his arms.

Love match

What a tiny thing to take one's heart
as hostage.

A kitten can hold thirty years
of friendship in his gift –
or a little, little time.
But, long or short, his life
will alter yours
and leave a lasting sorrow
when he leaves –
and a lasting gratitude.

One small cat changes
coming home to an empty house
to coming home.

Lessons
in life

MANKIND
TAKES ITSELF TOO SERIOUSLY.
KITTENS
ARE A MOST EFFECTIVE CURE.

KITTENS UNDERMINE POMPOSITY.

Kittens teach us humans wisdom
* – to delight in the moment*
* – to find joy in little things*
* – to value love and home*
*   – to enjoy adventure*
* – to face trouble bravely*
* – to know when to run away*
* – to avoid wasteful speculation*
but to deal with things as they occur
* – to keep clean and neat in every*
*   situation.*

OLD LADIES, contrary to belief,
do not turn to cats
as substitutes for babies.
They turn to them because
they are cats.
Because, after a lifetime of dealing
with people, they find the company
of cats a great relief.
Cats being companionable and kind,
discreet in their infidelities, courteous
in their dictatorial demands, delicate
in their greed, clean, beautiful and
elegant – even at their most ridiculous.
And vulnerable – as are we all.

So much fails with age – but a
kitten's beauty and his ingenuity
increase with every passing year.
However old a cat becomes,
his heart is young.
He holds his kitten self until the end.
As we do, in our human way.

If there are no kittens and no cats in
heaven, I refuse to go.